train of song, that echoes as

ur voice again. The sun is br

ove is ever true. The sky is b

ontent because of you. Becau

nd there runs a soft refrain

I soon shall hear your voic

because I know your love

oor, and I am well content

PRESENTED TO

FROM

DATE

Love Poems for Her

Watercolors by
Glenda Puhek

Ideals Publications
Nashville, Tennessee

ISBN 0-8249-5856-X

Published by Ideals Publications
A division of Guideposts
535 Metroplex Drive, Suite 250
Nashville, Tennessee 37211
www.idealsbooks.com

Color separations by Precision Color Graphics, Franklin, Wisconsin
Printed and bound in Italy

Library of Congress Cataloging-in-Publication Data

Love poems for her / watercolors by Glenda Puhek.
p. cm.
"Poems selected by Peggy Schaefer."
ISBN 0-8249-5856-X (alk. paper)
1. Love poetry. I. Puhek, Glenda. II. Schaefer, Peggy
PN6110.L6L495 2003
808.81'93543--dc21

2003007063

10 9 8 7 6 5 4 3 2 1

Poems Selected by Peggy Schaefer
Series Design by Eve DeGrie
Book Design by Jenny Eber Hancock

ACKNOWLEDGMENTS

CAMPBELL, CLARENCE B. "Tell Me of Your Love." Used by permission of Ray Campbell. GIOVANNI, NIKKI. "A Poem of Friendship." From *Love Poems*. Copyright © 1968-1997 by Nikki Giovanni. Published by William Morrow and Company. Reprinted by permission of HarperCollins Publishers Inc. HILLEMANN, ELEANOR. "To the One I Love." Used by permission of the author.

(continued on p. 88)

Contents

A New Love 6

The Beauty of Love 22

I Love You So 38

My Love Endures 58

Love Me True 72

A New Love

La Vita Nuova

In that book which is
My memory . . .
On the first page
That is the chapter when
I first met you
Appear the words . . .
Here begins a new life.

—Dante Alighieri

A Portrait

She was a phantom of delight
When first she gleamed upon my sight—
A lovely apparition, sent
To be a moment's ornament.
Her eyes as stars of twilight fair;
Like twilight's, too, her dusky hair;
But all things else about her drawn
From May-time and the cheerful dawn;
A dancing shape, an image gay,
To haunt, to startle and waylay.

I saw her upon nearer view,
A spirit, yet a woman too!
Her household motions light and free,
And steps of virgin liberty;
A countenance in which did meet
Sweet records, promises as sweet;
A creature not too bright or good
For human nature's daily food;
For transient sorrows, simple wiles,
Praise, blame, love, kisses, tears, and smiles.

And now I see with eye serene
The very pulse of the machine;
A being breathing thoughtful breath,
A traveler 'twixt life and death;
The reason firm, the temperate will,
Endurance, foresight, strength, and skill;
A perfect woman, nobly planned,
To warn, to comfort and command;
And yet a spirit still, and bright
With something of an angel light.

—William Wordsworth

First Love

I ne'er was struck before that hour
With love so sudden and so sweet.
Her face, it bloomed like a sweet flower
And stole my heart away complete.

I never saw so sweet a face
As that I stood before.
My heart has left its dwelling place
And can return no more.

—John Clare

You Came as a Thought

when I was past such thinking
you came as a song when I had

finished singing you came when
the sun had just begun its set-

ting you were my evening star.
—J. Laughlin

Did Not

'Twas a new feeling—something more
Than we had dared to own before,
    Which then we hid not;
We saw it in each other's eye,
And wished, in every half-breathed sigh,
    To speak, but did not.

She felt my lips' impassioned touch—
'Twas the first time I dared so much,
    And yet she chid me not;
But whispered o'er by burning brow,
"Oh, do you doubt I love you now?"
    Sweet soul! I did not.

Warmly I felt her bosom thrill,
I pressed it closer, closer still,
    Though gently bid not;
Till—oh! the world hath seldom heard
Of lovers, who so nearly erred,
    And yet, who did not.

—Thomas Moore

THE FIRST DAY

I wish I could remember the first day,
First hour, first moment of your meeting me;
If bright or dim the season, it might be
Summer or winter for aught I can say.
So unrecorded did it slip away,
So blind was I to see and to foresee,
So dull to mark the budding of my tree
That would not blossom yet for many a May.
If only I could recollect it! Such
A day of days! I let it come and go
As traceless as a thaw of bygone snow.
It seemed to mean so little, meant so much!
If only now I could recall that touch,
First touch of hand in hand—did one but know!

—CHRISTINA ROSSETTI

In a Single Stroke

I have loved you, dear one,
Since the beginning of time . . .
Before the stone age,
Before the seas were made.

Your arms close about me
And the circle is my world.
I was always there;
All other memories fade.

I have no other need.
You are the seed and the tree.
You are my body's shield;
You are the comforting cloak.

You are the calm of my soul.
You are my answered prayer.
You are my here and hereafter
All in a single stroke.

—MARIE DEWINSTANLEY PARKS

FIRST SHOWN

With you first shown to me,
With you first known to me,
My lifetime loom'd, in hope, a length of joy:
Your voice so sweetly spoke,
Your mind so meetly spoke,
My hopes were all of bliss without alloy,
As I, for your abode, sought out, with pride,
This house with vines o'er-ranging all its side.

I thought of years to come,
All free of tears to come,
When I might call you mine, and mine alone,
With steps to fall for me,
And day cares all for me,
And hands forever nigh to help my own;
And then thank'd him who had not cast my time
Too early or too late for your sweet prime.

—WILLIAM BARNES

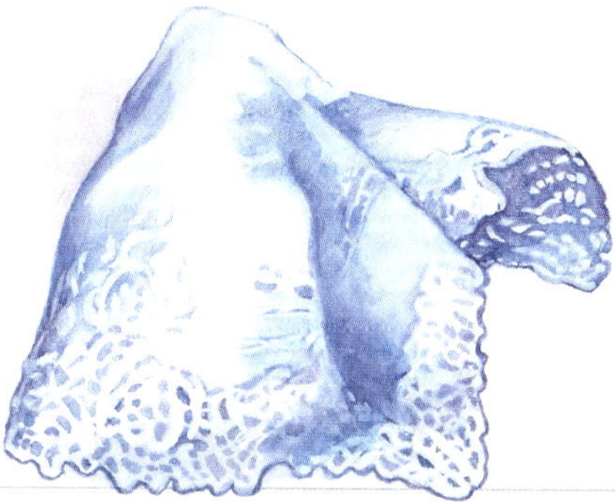

THE BEAUTY OF LOVE

THINE EYES STILL SHINED

Thine eyes still shined for me, though far
I lonely roved the land or sea:
As I behold yon evening star,
Which yet beholds not me.

This morn I climbed the misty hill
And roamed the pastures through;
How danced thy form before my path
Amidst the deep-eyed dew!

When the redbird spread his sable wing,
And showed his side of flame;
When the rosebud ripened to the rose,
In both I read thy name.

—RALPH WALDO EMERSON

Cherry-Ripe

There is a garden in her face
  Where roses and white lilies blow;
A heavenly paradise is that place,
  Wherein all pleasant fruits do flow:
    There cherries grow which none may buy
    Till "Cherry-ripe" themselves do cry.

Those cherries fairly do enclose
  Of orient pearls a double row,
Which when her lovely laughter shows,
  They look like rosebuds filled with snow;
    Yet them nor peer nor prince can buy
    Till "Cherry-ripe" themselves do cry.

Her eyes like angels watch them still;
  Her brows like bended bows do stand,
Threatening with piercing frowns to kill
  All that attempt with eye or hand
    Those sacred cherries to come nigh,
    Till "Cherry-ripe" themselves do cry.

—Thomas Campion

Night Thoughts

Stars, you are unfortunate, I pity you,
Beautiful as you are, shining in your glory,
Who guide seafaring men through stress and peril
And have no recompense from gods or mortals,
Love you do not, nor do you know what love is.
Hours that are aeons urgently conducting
Your figures in a dance through the vast heaven,
What journey have you ended in this moment,
Since lingering in the arms of my beloved
I lost all memory of you and midnight.

—Johann Wolfgang von Goethe

She Walks in Beauty

She walks in beauty, like the night
Of cloudless climes and starry skies;
And all that's best of dark and bright
Meet in her aspect and her eyes:
Thus mellowed to that tender light
Which heaven to gaudy day denies.

One shade the more, one ray the less,
Had half impaired the nameless grace
Which waves in every raven tress,
Or softly lightens o'er her face;
Where thoughts serenely sweet express
How pure, how dear their dwelling place.

And on that cheek, and o'er that brow,
So soft, so calm, yet eloquent,
The smiles that win, the tints that glow,
But tell of days in goodness spent,
A mind at peace with all below,
A heart whose love is innocent!

—LORD BYRON

My Lady's Presence Makes the Roses Red

My lady's presence makes the roses red,
Because to see her lips they blush for shame.
The lily's leaves, for envy, pale became,
And her white hands in them this envy bred.
The marigold the leaves abroad doth spread,
Because the sun's and her power is the same.
The violet of purple color came
Dyed in the blood she made my heart to shed.

In brief: all flowers from her their virtue take;
From her sweet breath their sweet smells do
    proceed;
The living heat which her eyebeams doth make
Warmeth the ground and quickeneth the seed.
The rain, wherewith she watereth the flowers,
Falls from mine eyes, which she dissolves in
    showers.

—HENRY CONSTABLE

Changeful Beauty

Whether I find thee bright with fair,
Or still as bright with raven hair;
With equal grace thy tresses shine,
Ah, queen, and Love will dwell divine
In these thy locks, on that far day,
When gold or sable turns to gray!

—Andrew Lang

Shall I Compare Thee?

Shall I compare thee to a summer's day?
Thou art more lovely and more temperate.
Rough winds do shake the darling buds of May,
And summer's lease hath all too short a date:
Sometimes too hot the eye of heaven shines,
And often is his gold complexion dimm'd;
And every fair from fair sometimes declines,
By chance, or nature's changing course untrimmed;

But thy eternal summer shall not fade,
Nor lose possession of that fair thou ow'st,
Nor shall death brag thou wander'st in his shade,
When in eternal lines to time thou grow'st;
    So long as men can breathe, or eyes can see,
    So long lives this, and this gives life to thee.

—William Shakespeare

To Helen

Helen, thy beauty is to me
    Like those Nicéan barks of yore,
That gently, o'er a perfumed sea,
    The weary, way-worn wanderer bore
    To his own native shore.

On desperate seas long wont to roam,
    Thy hyacinth hair, thy classic face,
Thy Naiad airs have brought me home
    To the glory that was Greece,
    And the grandeur that was Rome.

Lo! in yon brilliant window-niche
    How statue-like I see thee stand,
The agate lamp within thy hand!
    Ah, Psyche, from the regions which
    Are Holy Land!

—Edgar Allan Poe

I Love You So

A White Rose

The red rose whispers of passion,
And the white rose breathes of love;
Oh, the red rose is a falcon,
And the white rose is a dove.

But I send you a cream-white rosebud,
With a flush on its petal tips;
For the love that is purest and sweetest
Has a kiss of desire on its lips.

—John Boyle O'Reilly

Why Do I Love You?

I love you,
Not only for what you are,
But for what I am
When I am with you.

I love you,
Not only for what
You have made of yourself,
But for what
You are making of me.

I love you
For ignoring the possibilities
Of the fool in me
And for laying firm hold
Of the possibilities for good.

Why do I love you?

I love you
For closing your eyes
To the discords —
And for adding to the music in me
By worshipful listening.

I love you because you
Are helping me to make
Of the lumber of my life
Not a tavern
But a temple;
And out of the words
Of my every day,
Not a reproach
But a song.

I love you
Because you have done
More than any creed
To make me happy.

You have done it
Without a word,
Without a touch,
Without a sign.
You have done it
Just by being yourself.

After all,
Perhaps that is what
Love means.

—Roy Croft

An Hour with Thee

An hour with thee! When earliest day
Dapples with gold the eastern gray.
Oh, what can frame my mind to bear
The toil and turmoil, cark and care,
New griefs, which coming hours unfold,
And sad remembrance of the old?
    One hour with thee.

One hour with thee! When burning June
Waves her red flag at pitch of noon;
What shall repay the faithful swain
His labor on the sultry plain;
And, more than cave or sheltering bough,
Cool feverish blood and throbbing brow?
    One hour with thee.

One hour with thee! When sun is set,
Oh, what can teach me to forget
The thankless labors of the day;
The hopes, the wishes, flung away;
The increasing wants, and lessening gains,
The master's pride, who scorns my pains?
  One hour with thee.

—Sir Walter Scott

I Forget All Time

With thee conversing, I forget all time,
All seasons, and their change; all please alike.
Sweet is the breath of morn, her rising sweet,
With charm of earliest birds; pleasant the sun,
When first on this delightful land he spreads
His orient beams, on herb, tree, fruit, and flower
Glistering with dew; fragrant the fertile earth
After soft showers, and sweet the coming-on
Of grateful evening mild; then silent night,
With this her solemn bird, and this fairy moon,
And these the gems of Heaven, her starry train.

But neither breath of morn, when she ascends
With charm of earliest birds; nor rising sun
On this delightful land; nor herbs, fruit, flower
Glistering with dew; nor frangrance after showers;
Nor grateful evening mild; nor silent night,
With this her solemn bird; nor walk by moon,
Or glittering star-light, without thee is sweet.

—John Milton

A Poem of Friendship

We are not lovers
because of the love
we make
but the love
we have

We are not friends
because of the laughs
we spend
but the tears
we save

I don't want to be near you
for the thoughts we share
but the words we never have
to speak

I will never miss you
because of what we do
but what we are
together

—Nikki Giovanni

A Soft Refrain

Because of you my heart is glad today,
And through my mind there runs a soft refrain
Of song, that echoes as I work or play,
Because I soon shall hear your voice again.
The sun is brighter than it was before,
Because I know your love is ever true.
The sky is bluer through the open door,
And I am well content because of you.

Now, ever in my heart, there seems to be
An aim, an ardent wish, a constant prayer
That any place my duty beckons me,
That you'll be ever faithful, near me there;
That through the mist of swiftly passing years,
Your love will still remain so tried and true;
That I can wait and laugh at all my fears
And whisper, "I'm content," because of you.

—EUNICE ELMORE HEIZER

I Love You

I love you for what you are, but I love you
yet more for what you are going to be.
I love you not so much for your realities
as for your ideals.
I pray for your desires that they may be great,
rather than for your satisfactions,
which may be so hazardously little.
You are going forward toward something great.
I am on the way with you,
and therefore I love you.

—Carl Sandburg

Tell Me of Your Love

I could not do so in a thousand years,
A thousand years of happiness and tears.
And if each year could boast a thousand days,
And each day show a thousand different ways
To speak my thoughts in every language known,
Elaborating on this theme alone,
I could not make you understand what lies
Beyond all understanding, what defies
Translation into any form of art.
I cannot brush the motions of my heart
On canvas, play them on the stage, display
Them in a case of words. I only pray
That sometime, at the edge of dreams, you may
Draw close to what I wish so much to say.

—Clarence B. Campbell

I Love Thee

I love thee, as I love the calm
Of sweet, star-lighted hours!
I love thee, as I love the balm
Of early jes'mine flow'rs.
I love thee, as I love the last
Rich smile of fading day,
Which lingereth, like the look we cast,
On rapture pass'd away.

—Eliza Acton

So Are You to My Thoughts

So are you to my thoughts as food to life,
Or as sweet-season'd showers are to the ground;
And for the peace of you I hold such strife
As 'twixt a miser and his wealth is found.
Now proud as an enjoyer, and anon
Doubting the filching age will steal his treasure;
Now counting best to be with you alone,
Then better'd that the world may see my pleasure:
Sometime all full with feasting on your sight,
And by and by clean starved for a look;
Possessing or pursuing no delight
Save what is had, or must from you be took.
  Thus do I pine and surfeit day by day,
  Or gluttoning on all, or all away.

—William Shakespeare

Because of You

Because of you
The floor of my heart
Is paved with sunbeams,
Warming every minute
Of every golden day.

The thermal robe
Of security
Clothes me, and the flowers
Of my memory
Never fade away.

Soft music fills
The velvet night
And peace enfolds my soul
Because of you!

—Marie deWinstanley Parks

My Love Endures

Believe Me, if All Those Endearing Young Charms

Believe me, if all those endearing young charms,
  Which I gaze on so fondly today,
Were to change by tomorrow, and fleet in my arms,
  Like fairy-gifts fading away,
Thou wouldst still be adored, as this moment thou art,
  Let thy loveliness fade as it will,
And around the dear ruin each wish of my heart
  Would entwine itself verdantly still.

—Thomas Moore

Enduring Love

My love for you grows deeper
As each year passes by;
I sometimes sit and contemplate
Upon the reasons why.

I love you for your gentleness
In things you do and say,
And for the thoughtfulness you show
A hundred times a day.

I love you for your courage
And your wisdom when you speak;
They give to me the inner strength
I need when I am weak.

Some grow old regretfully
But I will age with pride;
I'll keep my love forever true
And walk close by your side.

—Virginia Peace

The Years

Tonight I close my eyes and see
A strange procession passing me—
The years before I saw your face
Go by me with a wistful grace;
They pass, the sensitive, shy years,
As one who strives to dance, half blind with tears.

The years went by and never knew
That each one brought me nearer you;
Their path was narrow and apart
And yet it led me to your heart—
Oh, sensitive shy years, oh, lonely years,
That strove to sing with voices drowned in tears.

—Sara Teasdale

We Have Lived and Loved Together

We have lived and loved together
Through many changing years;
We have shared each other's gladness
And wept each other's tears;
I have known ne'er a sorrow
That was long unsoothed by thee;
For thy smiles can make a summer
Where darkness else would be.

Like the leaves that fall around us
In autumn's fading hours,
Are the traitor's smiles, that darken
When the cloud of sorrow lowers;

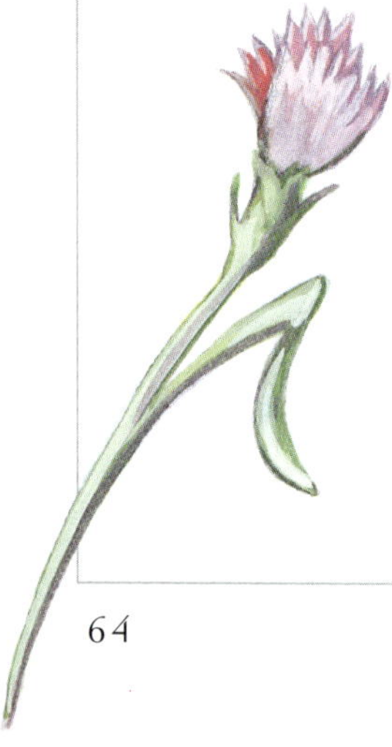

And though many such we've known, love,
  Too prone, alas, to range,
We both can speak of one love
  Which time can never change.

We have lived and loved together
  Through many changing years;
We have shared each other's gladness
  And wept each other's tears.
And let us hope the future
  As the past has been will be:
I will share with thee my sorrows,
  And thou thy joys with me.

—Charles Jefferys

To the One I Love

I can think of nothing better
Than the years ahead with you;
Of walking down the path of life,
And making dreams come true.

I can think of nothing sweeter
Than to have you by my side,
To cherish you forever,
And in your heart abide.

There's a precious bit of heaven
In your eyes whene'er you smile,
And it makes me very happy
Just to be with you the while.

I can hear the angels singing
When you whisper words of love,
And I thank my God in Heaven
For his precious gift of love.

—ELEANOR HILLEMANN

SHOULD YOU GO FIRST

Should you go first and I remain
　　To finish with the scroll,
No length'ning shadows shall creep in
　　To make this love seem droll.
We've known so much of happiness,
　　We've had our cup of joy,
And memory is one gift of God
　　That death cannot destroy.

—ALBERT ROWSWELL

Evening Song

Look off, dear Love, across the sallow sands,
And mark yon meeting of the sun and sea;
How long they kiss in sight of all the lands,
Ah! longer, longer we.

Now, in the sea's red vintage melts the sun,
As Egypt's pearl dissolved in rosy wine,
And Cleopatra-night drinks all — 'tis done,
Love, lay thine hand in mine.

Come forth, sweet stars, and comfort heaven's heart,
Glimmer, ye waves, round else unlighted sands;
Oh night! divorce our sun and sky apart—
Never our lips, our hands.

—Sidney Lanier

Love Me True

Love Me Not

Love not me for comely grace,
For my pleasing eye or face;
Nor for any outward part,
No, not for my constant heart:
For those may fail or turn to ill,
So thou and I shall sever.
Keep therefore a true woman's eye,
And love me still, but know not why;
So hast thou the same reason still
To dote upon me ever.

—John Wilbye

Beautiful Dreamer

Beautiful dreamer, wake unto me,
Starlight and dewdrops are waiting for thee;
Sounds of the rude world heard in the day,
Lull'd by the moonlight, have all pass'd away!

Beautiful dreamer, queen of my song,
List while I woo thee with soft melody;
Gone are the cares of life's busy throng—
Beautiful dreamer, awake unto me!

Beautiful dreamer, out on the sea
Mermaids are chanting the wild lorelie;
Over the streamlet vapors are borne,
Waiting to fade at the bright coming morn.

Beautiful dreamer, beam on my heart,
E'en as the morn on the streamlet and sea;
Then will all clouds of sorrow depart—
Beautiful dreamer, awake unto me!

—STEPHEN FOSTER

I Fear Thy Kisses

I fear thy kisses, gentle maiden;
Thou needest not fear mine;
My spirit is too deeply laden
Ever to burden thine.

I fear thy mien, thy tones, thy motion;
Thou needest not fear mine;
Innocent is the heart's devotion
With which I worship thine.

—P. B. Shelley

If I Should Give My Heart

If I should give my heart to you,
Would you share love with me—
The music of a bubbling brook,
The leafing of a tree?

Would you be just and grant to me
The ecstasies of sight—
The rainbow on a sun-lit cloud,
The grace of birds in flight?

Would you be kind and let me hear
The bells atop the spire,
The whippoorwill, the sighing breeze,
The crackling of a fire—

If I should give my heart to you?

—Gloria A. Martin

Love's Trinity

Soul, heart, and body, we thus singly name,
Are not in love divisible and distinct,
But each with each inseparably link'd.
One is not honor, and the other shame,
But burn as closely fused as fuel, heat, and flame.
They do not love who give the body and keep
The heart ungiven; nor they who yield the soul,
And guard the body. Love doth give the whole;
Its range being high as heaven, as ocean deep,
Wide as the realms of air or planet's curving sweep.

—Alfred Austin

The Passionate Shepherd to His Love

Come live with me and be my love,
And we will all the pleasures prove,
That hills and valleys, dales and fields,
Or woods or steepy mountain yields.

And we will sit upon the rocks,
And see the shepherds feed their flocks
By shallow rivers, to whose falls
Melodious birds sing madrigals.

And I will make thee beds of roses
And a thousand fragrant posies;
A cap of flowers, and a kirtle
Embroidered all with leaves of myrtle.

A gown made of the finest wool,
Which from our pretty lambs we pull;
Fair linéd slippers for the cold,
With buckles of the purest gold.

A belt of straw and ivy-buds,
With coral clasps and amber studs:
And if these pleasures may thee move,
Come live with me and be my love.

The shepherd swains shall dance and sing
For thy delight each May morning:
If these delights thy mind may move,
Then live with me and be my love.

—CHRISTOPHER MARLOWE

Of Pearls and Stars

The pearly treasures of the sea,
The lights that spatter heaven above,
More precious than these wonders are
My heart-of-hearts filled with your love.

The ocean's power, the heavenly sights
Cannot outweigh a love-filled heart.
And sparkling stars or glowing pearls
Pale as love flashes, beams and darts.

So, little, youthful maiden, come
Into my ample, feverish heart
For heaven and earth and sea and sky
Do melt as love has melt my heart.

—Heinrich Heine

Title Index

Beautiful Dreamer, 74
Because of You, 57
Believe Me, if All Those Endearing Young Charms, 59
Changeful Beauty, 32
Cherry-Ripe, 24
Did Not, 14
Enduring Love, 60
Evening Song, 70
First Day, The, 17
First Love, 12
First Shown, 20
Hour with Thee, An, 44
If I Should Give My Heart, 78
I Fear Thy Kisses, 76
I Forget All Time, 46
I Love You, 52
I Love Thee, 54
In a Single Stroke, 18
La Vita Nuova, 7
Love Me Not, 73
Love's Trinity, 81
My Lady's Presence Makes the Roses Red, 30
Night Thoughts, 27
Passionate Shepherd to His Love, The, 82
Pearls and Stars, Of, 84
Poem of Friendship, A, 49
Portrait, A, 8
Shall I Compare Thee?, 34
She Walks in Beauty, 28
Should You Go First, 69
So Are You to My Thoughts, 56
Soft Refrain, A, 50
Tell Me of Your Love, 53
Thine Eyes Still Shined, 23
To Helen, 36
To the One I Love, 66
We Have Lived and Loved Together, 64
White Rose, 39
Why Do I Love You?, 40
Years, The, 62
You Came as a Thought, 13

Author Index

Acton, Eliza, 54
Austin, Alfred, 81
Barnes, William, 20
Byron, Lord, 28
Campbell, Clarence B., 53
Campion, Thomas, 24
Clare, John, 12
Constable, Henry, 30
Croft, Roy, 40
Dante Alighieri, 7
Emerson, Ralph Waldo, 23
Foster, Stephen, 74
Giovanni, Nikki, 49
Goethe, Johann Wolfgang von, 27
Heine, Heinrich, 84
Heizer, Eunice Elmore, 50
Hillemann, Eleanor, 66
Jefferys, Charles, 64
Lang, Andrew, 32
Lanier, Sidney, 70
Laughlin, J., 13
Marlowe, Christopher, 82
Martin, Gloria A., 78
Milton, John, 46
Moore, Thomas, 14, 59
O'Reilly, John Boyle, 39
Parks, Marie deWinstanley, 18, 57
Peace, Virginia, 60
Poe, Edgar Allan, 36
Rossetti, Christina, 17
Rowswell, Albert, 69
Sandburg, Carl, 52
Scott, Sir Walter, 44
Shakespeare, William, 34, 56
Shelley, P. B., 76
Teasdale, Sara, 62
Wilbye, John, 73
Wordsworth, William, 8

First Line Index

An hour with thee! When earliest day, 44
Beautiful dreamer, wake unto me, 74
Because of you, 57
Because of you my heart is glad today, 50
Believe me, if all those endearing young charms, 59
Come live with me and be my love, 82
Helen, thy beauty is to me, 36
I can think of nothing better, 66
I could not do so in a thousand years, 53
I fear thy kisses, gentle maiden, 76
I have loved you, dear one, 18
If I should give my heart to you, 78
I love thee, as I love the calm, 54
I love you, 40
I love you for what you are, but I love you, 52
I ne'er was struck before that hour, 12
In that book which is, 7
I wish I could remember the first day, 17
Look off, dear Love, across the sallow sands, 70
Love not me for comely grace, 73
My lady's presence makes the roses red, 30
My love for you grows deeper, 60
Shall I compare thee to a summer's day?, 34
She walks in beauty, like the night, 28
She was a phantom of delight, 8
Should you go first and I remain, 69
So are you to my thoughts as food to life, 56
Soul, heart, and body, we thus singly name, 81

Stars, you are unfortunate, I pity you, 27
The pearly treasures of the sea, 84
The red rose whispers of passion, 39
There is a garden in her face, 24
Thine eyes still shined for me, though far, 23
Tonight I close my eyes and see, 62
'Twas a new feeling—something more, 14
We are not lovers, 49
We have lived and loved together, 64
when I was past such thinking, 13
Whether I find thee bright with fair, 32
With thee conversing, I forget all time, 46
With you first shown to me, 20

ACKNOWLEDGMENTS *(continued from p. 4)*

LAUGHLIN, JAMES. "You Came as a Thought" from *The Collected Poems of James Laughlin*. Copyright © 1938–1994 by James Laughlin. Used by permission of New Directions Publishing Corp., agents. Our sincere thanks to the following authors whom we were unable to contact: Roy Croft for "Why Do I Love You?"; Eunice Elmore Heizer for "A Soft Refrain"; Gloria A. Martin for "If I Should Give My Heart"; Marie deWinstanley Parks for "In a Single Stroke" and "Because of You"; Virginia Peace for "Enduring Love"; Albert Kennedy Rowswell for "Should You Go First" from *Rosey Reflections*, by Albert K. Rowswell, 1945.

While every effort has been made to establish ownership and use of each selection in this book, this has not always been possible. If contacted, the publisher will be pleased to rectify any inadvertent errors or omissions in subsequent editions.

refrain of song, That echoes

your voice again. The sun is

love is ever true. The sky

ll content because of you. B

mind there runs a soft refra

use I soon shall hear your

ore, because I know your lo

n door, and I am well cont

t refrain of song, that echoe

ar your voice again. The sun

ur love is ever true. The sky

ll content because of you.

y mind there runs a soft ref

cause I soon shall hear your

fore, because I know your

en door, and I am well con